PACIFIC CREST TRAIL
A JOURNEY IN PHOTOGRAPHS

CHRIS ALEXANDER

Pacific Crest Trail: A Journey in Photographs
Photography by Chris Alexander
Production by Anna Sofranko

wanderingthewild.com

chrisalexanderphoto.com
chris@chrisalexanderphoto.com

Copyright © 2013 Chris Alexander

All rights reserved. No part of this publication may be reproduced or transmitted in any form or by any means, electronic or mechanical, including photocopy, recording, or any information storage and retrieval system, without permission in writing from the author.

ISBN: 978-0-615-74109-3

Printed by The Avery Group at Shapco Printing, Inc., Minneapolis

ACKNOWLEDGEMENTS

My partner Anna Sofranko worked side by side with me on this book from beginning to end. Her project management, caption research, design ideas, editing, and assistance on every aspect of the book has been invaluable. I cannot thank her enough.

Anna and I experienced the fundamental goodness of people during our Pacific Crest Trail thru hike and the creation of this book. We would especially like to thank Jim and Cindy Sofranko for mailing our food resupply and replacement gear packages, Steve Quinn for creating the map on page 4, David Schmidt for sharing his vast knowledge of West Coast flora, Jen and Tim Christion Myers for fulfilling book orders, and Noah Beil for enlightening discussion of photography.

Thank you to the kind strangers (known as "trail angels" in the hiking community) who went out of their way to give us rides to the post office, offered us a place to shower and spend the night, filled water caches, and much more: Barney "Scout" and Sandy "Frodo" Mann, Lon "Half Mile" Cooper, Tristan, Pinkie, Dead Animal, Tom Figueroa, Herk McClellan, Katie Bolin, Amanda "Shepherd" Silvestri, Frank Valenzuela, Paul Woodruff, Lloyd and Juanita Sawchuk, Donna and Jeff Saufley, Christy "Rockin", Dan, and Grant Rosander, Golden Boy, Okie Girl, The Owl, Lori and Joe near Carson Pass, Peggy and Steve Porto, Ken "Half Slow" Tran, Natalie, John, and Jason with the RV, Brenda and Laurie Braaten, Meridith "Piper's Mom" Rosendahl, Tread Lightly, "Subway Steve" Robbins, Barbara and Rick Zumbrun, Becky Alexander, Karin Graves, Dante Rodriguez and crew, Keith Wipple, Eric "Balls", Reed "Sunshine", and Annika "Butterfly" Gjonnes, Debbie Holcombe, Erin "Wired" Saver, Craig Giffen, Stephen Chan, Not Phil's Dad, David "White Jeep" Lippke, Andrea and Jerry Dinsmore, Chuck, Gondo, and many others who have assisted hikers throughout the years.

Also, thanks to our family and friends who shared their homes with us while we created this book: Jan and George Alexander, Christine and John Willig, Rich Sofranko, Jim and Cindy Sofranko, Jen and Tim Christion Myers, Elif Ertekin, Lucas Wagner, and Andrea Duran.

Finally, a hearty thanks to the Pacific Crest Trail Association and all its volunteers for maintaining this remarkable trail.

For Anna,
my partner
in adventure
and in life.

This book
would not exist
without you.

PACIFIC CREST TRAIL MAP

INTRODUCTION

In 2012, my partner Anna Sofranko and I walked the entire 2660-mile Pacific Crest Trail. The trail begins at the US/Mexican border, stretches through California, Oregon, and Washington, and ends at the Canadian border. Despite blisters, bears, fatigue, shin splints, and swarms of mosquitoes, the spectacular scenery at every turn inspired us to keep walking. We traversed 24 national forests and 7 national parks, rarely encountering civilization. The map at left shows our full route. As we hiked, we documented our personal experiences on our website, wanderingthewild.com. After the hike, we created this book to showcase my best images of the trail's incredible landscapes.

Over 75 years before we set foot on the Pacific Crest Trail, teams of young men from the YMCA first scouted its route. Clinton C. Clarke and Warren Rodgers urged the US government to create a hiking trail from Mexico to Canada. However, it wasn't until 1968 that the National Trails System Act officially established the Pacific Crest Trail. It was declared complete in 1993, but it is only through the constant efforts of volunteers and the Pacific Crest Trail Association that the trail remains continuous and walkable.

Our Pacific Crest Trail journey began on the morning of April 19, 2012. Nervous and excited, we started walking north from the Mexican border. In southern California, we crossed the starkly beautiful terrain of the Anza-Borrego and Mojave Deserts, rejoicing in spring's new growth. The Pacific Crest Trail, as its name implies, follows the crests of major mountain ranges along its route. Thus, even in the desert we completed serious climbs and were rewarded with panoramic views.

By early June, we reached the Sierra Nevada Mountains, which are world famous for their dramatic scenery. Snow still lingered at these higher elevations, and nighttime temperatures sometimes dropped below freezing. We climbed up and over mountain passes in Sequoia, Kings Canyon, and Yosemite National Parks, marveling at the turquoise and deep blue alpine lakes that lay below. It was amazing to camp in these pristine lands and to sleep under millions of stars.

Hiking continually north, we descended into the lower hills and forests of northern California. To reach Canada before autumn's snow blocked our path, we needed to walk an average of 20 miles each day. This pace was challenging to maintain, testing our resolve on a regular basis. But covering so much ground ensured we saw incredible things every day, such as origami-like leopard lilies, a geothermal lake, and carnivorous pitcher plants.

After 110 days of walking in California, we celebrated our entry into Oregon. The terrain mellowed out a bit, the forest's canopy protected us from summer's heat, and the soft trail, carpeted with pine needles, was a treat for our feet. These densely forested sections periodically gave way to fields of black lava rocks and towering volcanoes. A highlight was walking the rim of Crater Lake, one of the deepest lakes in the world, contained in a collapsed volcano cone.

Washington proved a spectacular final stretch, with lush old growth forests, dramatic peaks, and foggy vistas. The trail grew especially steep through the jagged Cascade Mountains. As autumn's chill began to turn vine maples red and larch trees yellow, we felt like migrating animals nearing the end of our journey just before winter settled in for good.

We reached the Canadian border on September 29, after over five months on the trail. During the hike, fresh air, clean water, and open space had surrounded and sustained us. Our time on the trail put us in touch with the rhythm of the sun and seasons, awakened our senses to the subtleties of nature, and strengthened our deep primal connection with the wild. At the trail's end, we were excited to have accomplished our goal, but sad to leave the wilderness which had inspired us so profoundly.

We knew from the beginning of the hike that we wanted to share these wild places with others. However, much of what we encountered defied description. Where language failed us, we turned to images. The best of those images are collected here, in chronological order, spaced evenly throughout the trail's length. My photographs are presented with a minimum of visual editing in order to accurately portray the landscapes we experienced. We hope you enjoy this visual journey of the Pacific Crest Trail.

— Chris Alexander

CALIFORNIA

Mile 0 | Fence, Border between Mexico and the United States

Mile 25 | Oak grove, Cleveland National Forest

Mile 49 | Laguna Mountains, Cleveland National Forest

Mile 82 | Barrel Cactus, Anza-Borrego Desert State Park

Mile 123 | Sun bleached branch, Cleveland National Forest

Mile 131 | Lizard on rock, Anza-Borrego Desert State Park

Mile 170 | Trail on ridge, San Jacinto Wilderness

Mile 211 | Fuller Ridge, San Gorgonio Pass

Mile 227 | Desert stream, San Gorgonio Wilderness

Mile 236 | Moon over burned trees, San Gorgonio Wilderness

Mile 238 | Manzanita, San Bernardino National Forest

Mile 277 | Tree on lichen covered rock, San Bernardino National Forest

Mile 324 | California poppies, San Bernardino National Forest

Mile 346 | Trail rounds bend, San Bernardino National Forest

Mile 377 | Trail climbs Mt. Baden-Powell, Angeles National Forest

Mile 409 | Yucca, Angeles National Forest

Mile 418 | Field of scarlet buglers in burned forest, Angeles National Forest

Mile 476 | Ridges, Angeles National Forest

Mile 522 | Moonlit Joshua trees, Mojave Desert

Mile 546 | Barren tree, Mojave Desert

Mile 617 | Dry stream bed, Mojave Desert

Mile 628 | Weathered sagebrush roots, Mojave Desert

Mile 653 | Ridge in shadow, Owens Peak Wilderness

Mile 735 | Rock face, Golden Trout Wilderness

Mile 741 | Spiral trunk, Golden Trout Wilderness

Mile 773 | Pool in meadow, Sequoia National Park

Mile 780 | Ice, Kings Canyon National Park

Mile 807 | Pinchot Pass, Kings Canyon National Park

Mile 819 | Snowmelt stream, Kings Canyon National Park

Mile 838 | Helen Lake, Kings Canyon National Park

Mile 864 | Stars above upper Sallie Keyes Lake, John Muir Wilderness

Mile 866 | Marie Lake, John Muir Wilderness

Mile 904 | Balanced tree, Ansel Adams Wilderness

Mile 923 | Banner Peak and Thousand Island Lake, Ansel Adams Wilderness

Mile 929 | Cloud near Donohue Pass, Ansel Adams Wilderness

Mile 988 | Wilma Lake, Yosemite National Park

Mile 1013 | Deer crossing snow field, Toiyabe National Forest

Mile 1014 | Latopie Lake, Toiyabe National Forest

Mile 1037 | Evening sky, Carson-Iceberg Wilderness

Mile 1039 | Young fir, Carson-Iceberg Wilderness

Mile 1103 | Reflection in Heather Lake, Desolation Wilderness

Mile 1119 | Corn lily, Desolation Wilderness

Mile 1128 | Exposed roots, Tahoe National Forest

Mile 1135 | Lake Tahoe, Granite Chief Wilderness

Mile 1186 | Snow plant, Tahoe National Forest

Mile 1204 | Trail switchbacks, Tahoe National Forest

Mile 1226 | Checkerbloom, Plumas National Forest

Mile 1281 | Grassy lake, Bucks Lake Wilderness

Mile 1284 | Feather River Canyon, Bucks Lake Wilderness

Mile 1328 | Lichen covered trunks, Lassen National Forest

Mile 1353 | Boiling Springs Lake, Lassen Volcanic National Park

Mile 1394 | Mt. Shasta at sunrise, Lassen National Forest

Mile 1395 | Hat Creek Rim, Lassen National Forest

Mile 1411 | Teasel, Hat Creek Valley

Mile 1440 | Leopard lilies, Shasta National Forest

Mile 1475 | Trail on hillside, Shasta National Forest

Mile 1510 | Waterfall, Castle Crags Wilderness

Mile 1521 | Pitcher plants, Castle Crags Wilderness

Mile 1542 | Deadfall Lake, Shasta National Forest

Mile 1592 | Salmon Mountains at sunset, Klamath National Forest

Mile 1632 | Trail through meadow, Marble Mountain Wilderness

Mile 1647 | Madrone, Klamath National Forest

OREGON

Mile 1716 | Meadow and north face of Mt. Shasta, Klamath National Forest

Mile 1758 | Butterfly on thistle, Bureau of Land Management, Medford District

Mile 1775 | Mullein in volcanic rocks, Rogue River-Siskiyou National Forest

Mile 1776 | Trail through volcanic rocks, Rogue River-Siskiyou National Forest

Mile 1835 | Crater Lake, Crater Lake National Park

Mile 1838 | Snow patch, Crater Lake National Park

Mile 1851 | Trail through forest, Crater Lake National Park

Mile 1895 | Raindrops in Summit Lake, Deschutes National Forest

Mile 1950 | Morning in forest, Three Sisters Wilderness

Mile 1966 | South Sister, Three Sisters Wilderness

Mile 1981 | North Sister, Three Sisters Wilderness

Mile 2002 | Moonrise, Mt. Washington Wilderness

Mile 2026 | Fog, Mt. Jefferson Wilderness

Mile 2073 | Decomposing tree, Warm Springs Indian Reservation

Mile 2095 | Mt. Hood, Mt. Hood National Forest

Mile 2115 | Waterfalls, Mt. Hood Wilderness

Mile 2134 | Sedge, Mt. Hood National Forest

WASHINGTON

Mile 2175 | Lush forest, Gifford Pinchot National Forest

Mile 2191 | Panther Creek, Gifford Pinchot National Forest

Mile 2236 | Evening light in forest, Gifford Pinchot National Forest

Mile 2277 | Corn lilies surrounded by asters, Goat Rocks Wilderness

Mile 2281 | Peaks at sunset, Goat Rocks Wilderness

Mile 2285 | Trail on knife edge ridge, Goat Rocks Wilderness

Mile 2310 | Sinuous creek, William O. Douglas Wilderness

Mile 2329 | Rising mist on Dewey Lake, William O. Douglas Wilderness

Mile 2352 | Trail through Pacific silver fir, Norse Peak Wilderness

Mile 2390 | Frog in creek, Mt. Baker-Snoqualmie National Forest

Mile 2415 | Huckleberry in rock crevice, Alpine Lakes Wilderness

Mile 2445 | Meadow, Alpine Lakes Wilderness

Mile 2488 | Above Glasses Lake, Henry M. Jackson Wilderness

Mile 2518 | Cascading creek, Glacier Peak Wilderness

Mile 2530 | Glaciers and fog, Glacier Peak Wilderness

Mile 2550 | Suiattle River, Glacier Peak Wilderness

Mile 2555 | Forest in fog, Glacier Peak Wilderness

Mile 2572 | Vine maple in autumn, Glacier Peak Wilderness

Mile 2604 | Cutthroat Pass, Okanogan National Forest

Mile 2635 | Trail through larch trees, Pasayten Wilderness

Mile 2650 | Valley, Pasayten Wilderness

Mile 2660 | Clear-cut, Border between the United States and Canada